SUPER SMART THINKING

SOCIOLOGY MADE EASY

Written by
Laura Pountney

Enslow PUBLISHING

For Ellie, a lovely neighbour – L.P.

Published in 2027 by Enslow Publishing, LLC
2544 Clinton Street
Buffalo, NY 14224

First published in Great Britain in 2021 by Wayland

Editor: John Hort
Design and illustration: Collaborate Ltd

Printed in China

CPSIA compliance information: Batch #QS27ENS: For further information contact Enslow Publishing LLC, New York, New York at 1-800-398-2504.

Please visit our website, www.enslowpublishing.com. For a free color catalog of all our high-quality books, call toll free 1-800-398-2504 or fax 1-877-980-4454.

Cataloging-in-Publication Data

Names: Pountney, Laura.
Title: Sociology made easy / by Laura Pountney.
Description: Buffalo, NY : Enslow Publishing, 2027. | Series: Super smart thinking | Includes glossary and index.
Identifiers: ISBN 9781978549234 (pbk.) | ISBN 9781978549241 (library bound) | ISBN 9781978549258 (ebook)
Subjects: LCSH: Sociology--Juvenile literature.
Classification: LCC HM585.P696 2027 | DDC 301--dc23

CONTENTS

WHAT IS SOCIOLOGY?

Welcome to sociology! This is a fascinating subject that will change the way you think about the world around you. Sociology simply means the study of society.

WHAT IS SOCIETY?

Society is a group of people who live together. Society is usually organized into groups, called institutions, such as the family, religions, and government.

Sociologists explore the ways that society shapes the way that you think and act.

HOW DO WE LEARN TO BE PART OF A SOCIETY?

It doesn't happen overnight! People learn, literally, how to be human through a process known as **socialization**.

This is where a person learns how to behave "normally" and also what is seen as right and wrong. Socialization is a process that takes place throughout our lives, from the moment we are born until we die. Examples include:

LEARNING THE RIGHT TABLE MANNERS

LEARNING TO MAKE FRIENDS

LEARNING TO TALK

LEARNING TO RESPOND TO AUTHORITY

If you were not socialized, then what do you think would happen?

People might act in ways that are negative for society, leading to **anomie,** which is a French word for "normlessness."

Sociologists explore society, using their sociological imagination. They look for "the strange in the familiar." This means everyday actions and activities are examined carefully to reveal interesting assumptions and meanings.

HOW DID SOCIOLOGY BEGIN?

During the 19th century people became much more interested in studying biology, physics, chemistry (the natural sciences), and medicine. Scientific thinking was different from what came before it as it focused on what is called **empirical evidence**, which means you have to see proof or evidence for something to be true.

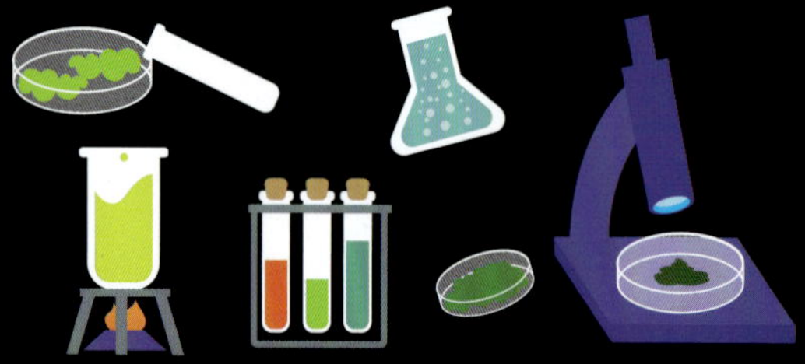

THE SCIENTIFIC APPROACH

Émile Durkheim (1858–1917) (left), a French sociologist, was determined to show that it was possible to use this scientific approach to explain changes in society over time.

Durkheim thought that sociology could help identify social problems, like **crime**, and use the scientific method to identify the causes. He argued that if the causes of crime were known, for example, you could solve the problem. He even argued that experiments could be used to study society.

DID YOU KNOW?

The word "sociology" was created by Auguste Comte (1798–1857), mixing the Latin term *societas*, meaning "companion," with the Greek word *logos*, which means "the study of."

CHANGING SOCIETY

Society changed quickly during the 19th century, and sociologists argued that they could help explain these changes. For example, during this period, families changed as many people left the countryside to live in cities – a process known as **urbanization**. Society got a lot more complex in a very short span of time!

While some sociologists saw the changes in society as positive, other sociologists were not so sure, arguing that the changes meant that some people ended up being more powerful than others. This group of sociologists was critical of the changes and called for a more equal, fair society.

And sociology was born! Sociologists all see the world very differently, so there is always lots of debate about social issues.

HOW DO SOCIOLOGISTS FIND OUT ABOUT PEOPLE'S LIVES?

Sociologists are not simply working in offices thinking about social issues. In fact, a really important part of their work is about getting out into the real world and carrying out social **research**.

This is because sociologists believe that you can't simply make statements about social issues, you need observable, or empirical, evidence to back up what you are saying.

So sociologists use a wide range of ways of finding out how people think and act, known as research methods. Some research methods involve counting and numbers, and other methods involve words and images.

Methods involving numbers produce **quantitative data**.

Methods involving words and images produce **qualitative data**.

QUANTITATIVE METHODS	QUALITATIVE METHODS
Numbers are used to understand social issues.	Words and images are used to understand social issues.
Experiments and questionnaires.	Watching people in their daily life. Observation and interviews allow people to relax and talk.
Research must focus on being reliable, which means you can repeat the research and get similar results.	The most important aim of research is to find the truth, so validity (truthfulness) is important.

UNDERCOVER RESEARCH

The type of research method you pick depends on what you are studying. So, for example, if you are studying burglars, it wouldn't really work if you asked them to fill in a questionnaire! Sociologists sometimes carry out undercover research. For instance, they may observe criminals with the help of police.

PRIMARY AND SECONDARY RESEARCH

If a researcher carries out research of their own, it is known as **primary research**. Sometimes sociologists find out about a social issue by using data or information that already exists, which is known as **secondary research**.

SOCIETY WORKS! FUNCTIONALIST IDEAS

Sociologists all see society differently. It is like looking at this image ... **What do you see?**

Some people see an old woman, while others see a young woman looking away.

Sociologists look at society in different ways, known as different "theories."

Theories are sets of ideas that explain change in society over time.

One of the earliest theories in sociology was **functionalism**. There is a clue in the name – it says society functions!

Functionalists are sociologists who are very positive about society. They believe it functions, or works, well and is good for every individual. They also believe that people need to feel like they are part of society by being socialized.

Functionalists see people as needing social forces to shape the way that they behave. In fact, they see people as being like puppets on a string.

For example, people need to be reminded what is "normal behavior," or **norms**, and also what is considered to be important in society, its **values**.

Functionalist thinkers, such as Durkheim, carried out important research to show **social facts** can be created. These, he argued, could be used to find answers to **social problems**.

FUNCTIONALISTS HAVE BEEN VERY IMPORTANT IN EXPLAINING THINGS LIKE ...

How families have changed over time, and what they do to keep society running smoothly.

Why school is important in preparing people to fit into society later in life.

Why crime happens and why it is important to remind us of what is right or wrong.

Why religion is important in society.

Some sociologists argue that functionalist views are SO positive that it means they overlook problems in society. And other sociologists argue that functionalists ideas are old-fashioned. Functionalist views, although still important, tended to be created by white men from Europe and North America and so don't really take into account other people's views, such as women, or people from different places or backgrounds.

WHO WAS MARX?

Karl Marx was born in Germany in 1818. His ideas would become so important that by 1920, large areas of the world were ruled under his ideas. His ideas continue to be important today.

MARX'S IDEA OF COMMUNISM

Marx disliked many of the changes he saw happening in Europe during his life, as people began to live in cities and work in factories. Marx thought that this type of work divided society into two groups, or **social classes**.

The two groups Marx identified were: the owners of factories (he called these the **ruling class**) and the people that worked in the factories, the workers, or **working class**. Marx hated the way that the ruling class paid the workers very little and kept all the profit for themselves, getting very rich.

Marx disliked this new system (known as **capitalism**) so much that he and some other thinkers of the time thought of a new type of society, which they thought was fairer and more equal. He called this **communism**.

In a communist society, the government makes sure that wealth is shared more equally, so that everyone has enough to eat, a house, and a job. Communist societies have existed in places all over the world, such as China, Cuba, Sudan, Nicaragua, and Kenya.

Communism sounds great, doesn't it?

But there were some problems. First of all, Marx (right) encouraged workers to have a **revolution** against the capitalist system, which wasn't always peaceful. Also, even in communist countries, some people were still eager to keep lots of money for themselves, as well as keeping the rest of society quite poor. So it turns out, people aren't very good at sharing after all!

FEMINISM: WOMEN IN SOCIOLOGY

In the past, women were not allowed to be educated as highly as men or weren't educated at all. Many women were not allowed to work and those who did could only do certain jobs. Feminists have long spoken up for women's rights, and in the 20th century, women started to gain more rights in many places.

Even in the 20th century, many women were expected to spend most of their time looking after the home and children. There were very few female sociologists. In the 1960s, some very important changes happened.

Feminist sociologists wrote important books and drew more attention to how they were (and still are) **oppressed** – or have less power than men – in what is called a **patriarchal** society. These feminists also marched, protested, and formed groups to call attention to women being discriminated against. Feminists demanded changes in the **law**, for example, to make sure men and women were paid the same amount for the same work. As a **social movement**, feminism achieved a huge amount of **social change** and continues to do so today.

FIGHTING FOR EQUALITY

Feminists know that women are not all the same. In fact, there are lots of types of feminists, all with different ideas with different thoughts about the solutions to fight the patriarchy.

Don't forget that anyone can be a feminist. In fact, anyone who thinks that men and women should be equal is a feminist!

Although there have been some really important signs of change, men and women are still not equal today in some areas of life, so the fight goes on!

WHY MEANINGS ARE IMPORTANT TOO

Functionalists and **Marxists** are interested in exploring and explaining changes in society by looking at the way social forces in society shape people's behavior. Not everyone agrees with this view. Max Weber (1864–1920), an important German sociologist, argued instead that to really understand society, it is important to look at the small details of everyday life.

WEBER AND THE CALVINISTS

Weber studied a group of Christians in Germany, called **Calvinists**. Calvinists were a group of people who believed in the religious ideas of a man called John Calvin (1509–1564), who wanted to change the way people thought about Christianity. Weber showed how small day-to-day changes in their lives led to massive changes in their society.

Weber concluded that day-to-day religious meanings are very important and tell us a lot about society.

These ideas were picked up by other sociologists, who developed ideas such as the **labeling theory**. This is where people decide what someone else is like by looking at the way they dress, act, or speak. In school, for example, a teacher might look at a pupil and decide they are good because they look neat and tidy, are polite, and are quiet.

These ideas became known as **social action theory**. The theory states that people have choices about how they act in society and aren't simply like puppets on a string, as functionalists and Marxists say.

RECENT WAYS OF EXPLAINING CHANGE: POSTMODERNISM

In the 1980s, a group of sociologists decided that the world had changed so much that the other ways of explaining the world were no longer useful. These sociologists are called **postmodernists**, which literally means beyond the "modern" period of life.

A NEW WORLDVIEW

Postmodernist ideas were not just emerging in sociology, they were also occurring in art, writing, and films. These ideas are all about understanding the world around us today, a world in which so many changes are happening all the time.

For example, in the past, or the modern era, people's lives tended to be more simple, with few changes, and people tended to share similar views about the world.

Think about family life. In the past, people usually married before they had children. Today there are lots of different ways of making a family. We have many more choices today about how to show different parts of our lives, our **identity**.

Today, as we travel much more and use computers and the internet to see other ways of life, we no longer share "set" ideas about how to live our lives. This is partly because people and ideas have become more connected, a process sociologists call **globalization**.

So, postmodernists argue that there is no longer one set of answers to life's questions. Instead, there are many truths and ways of understanding the world, and not one of these is better than the other.

Postmodernists are interested in describing the world we live in today, which is about choice, diversity, and celebrating differences!

GETTING SOCIOLOGICAL ABOUT THE FAMILY

Sociologists have always been interested in the role that the family plays in society, in other words, what the family *does*.

Functionalists argue that the family is positive and helps society run smoothly. It is a space where children can be socialized and adults are able to relax.

Marxists think that the family simply helps to prepare people for work. The mother helps get the children ready to be workers when they grow up – not a very positive view of family life!

Feminists see the traditional family as patriarchal, meaning male-dominated. They want to see the family change to become more equal.

Single-parent families: today, parents can choose to raise children alone.

Step-families: people divorce or separate, then marry again!

FAMILY STRUCTURES

In the past, it was more likely that the family was made up of a mom, dad, and children, known as the nuclear family. But in in the last 50 years, there have been huge changes to the ways that family structures (sizes and shapes) and relationships are formed.

Same-sex families: made up of same-sex couples and their children.

Extended families: people may live with relatives such as aunts, uncles, or grandparents.

Living apart together: some people may even live apart but still be in a relationship.

Our relatives, meaning those we are connected with by marriage or blood, are important. However, recently, sociologists have been interested in people who we see as family members, even if we are NOT related to them.

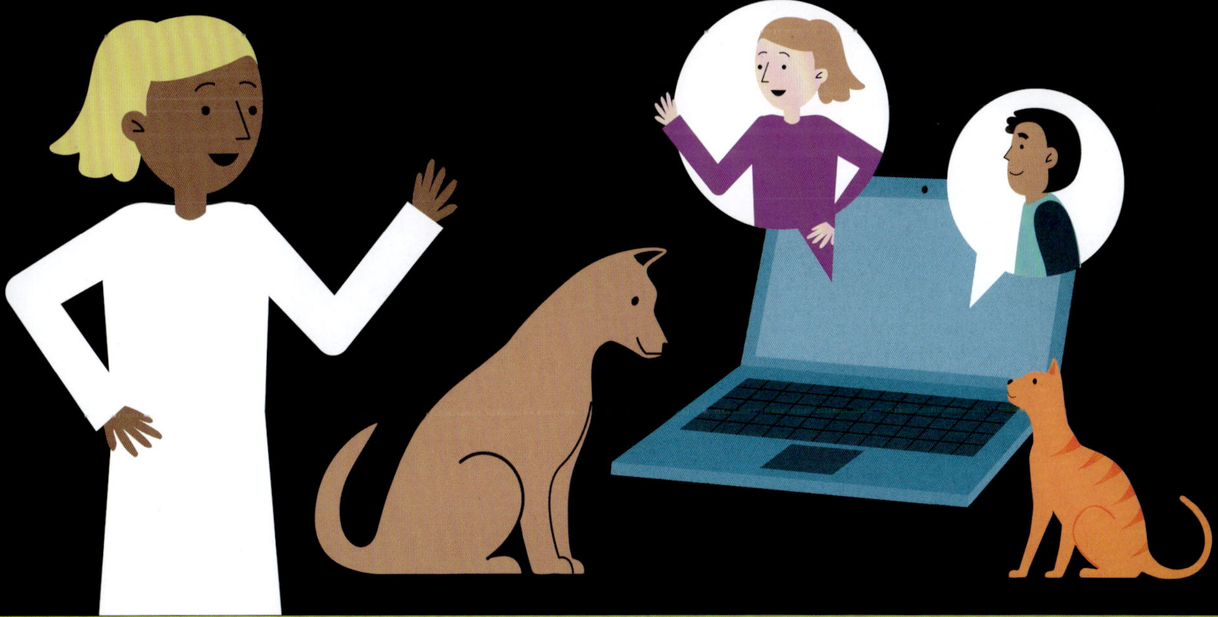

Sociologist are also interested in the ways that travel and the internet have led to new ways of organizing family life.

They are also interested in the changing nature of childhood, the effects of changes in the population **demography**, and changing laws that relate to family life.

WHY DO PEOPLE COMMIT CRIMES?

Sociologists like to explain why social problems happen. One example of this is crime, where people break the law. Ideas about what a "crime" is have changed over time and vary from place to place. Crime is a **social construct**, an idea built by society.

Functionalists argue that people commit crime when they have not been socialized properly. They even argue that some crime is a good thing, as this acts as a warning – showing the rest of society that change needs to happen. Functionalists also argue that we need crime to make sure people know the boundaries of society (a reminder of what is right and wrong).

Burglars are sent to jail for breaking rules.

Marxists argue that crime is another way that the ruling class get to control the working class. They say that the ruling class makes up the laws to remind the working class they have no power. Marxists also show how the powerful commit crimes and get away with them!

Feminists argue that women are often the victims of crime, and that society tends to encourage men to be violent and aggressive. They also think that if a woman carries out a crime, she is seen as **doubly deviant** for being a criminal *and* breaking the rules of being a woman!

Social action theorists argue that the police often label particular groups of people as criminals, so they are more likely to be stopped by the police.

Postmodernists argue that crime is not a very useful way of looking at bad or wrong behavior. They say we should look at the idea of "social harm" instead, figuring out the effects of crime rather than simply putting people in prison for breaking a law.

CRIME AND PUNISHMENT

Sociologists play an important role in checking the way that laws are used and the effects of crime. They also carry out research into the way the police do their jobs and explore who is likely to commit crime and who is likely to be a victim of crime.

Different people are more likely to commit certain crimes.

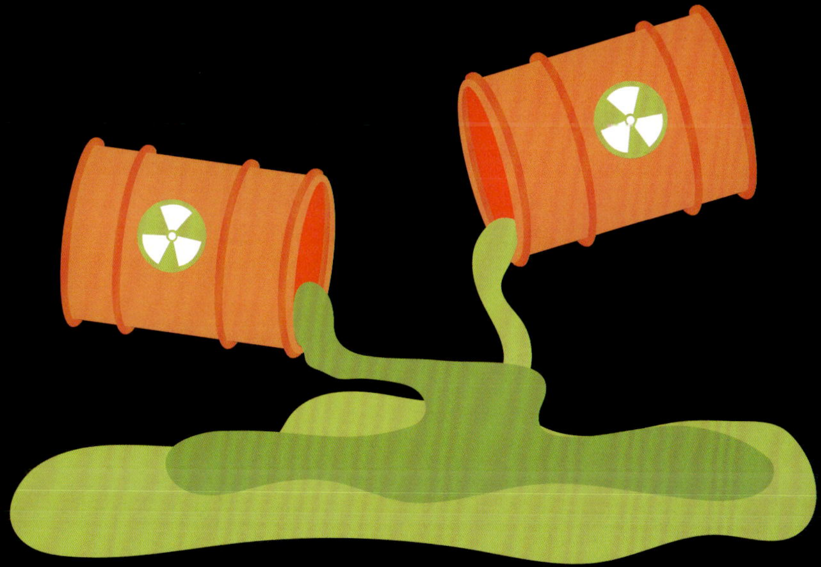

Sociologists also study new types of crimes that are happening, for example green crimes, which are crimes against the environment.

THE SOCIOLOGY OF THE CLASSROOM

The classroom is just where you learn, right? Sociologists disagree, arguing that it is where messages are transmitted to pupils.

Functionalists see these messages as positive, giving everyone the same chance to do well at school, so school is **meritocratic.**

Marxists disagree, arguing that education is where your social class is made very clear to you and those all around you. For example, they say that working-class pupils are less likely to do well at school if they are poor. Whereas middle-class pupils do well as they have not only money to pay for school trips, books, and private tutors, but they are also brought up into a set of ideas that make education easier. They argue that meritocracy is a myth, or a lie.

Feminists argue that although girls often get better grades than boys at school, they still get paid less later in life, partly because they are encouraged to take lower paid jobs.

Labeling theorists argue that teachers see some pupils as "ideal" and other pupils as less likely to do well. Through their research, sociologists have shown how powerful it is to be seen as, or labeled as, a "good student" or a "bad student." Students begin to believe their label, which can lead them to do well or badly.

LAW OF THE CLASSROOM

Recently, sociologist have been interested in the ways that changing laws have affected students' experiences and results at school. They are interested in the effects of **marketization**, which means that schools are being run like a business.

Test scores are very different among different groups of pupils, and sociologists are eager to investigate why this is the case. For example:

Working-class pupils get lower grades than middle-class pupils.

Boys get lower grades than girls.

Some **ethnic** groups do better than others in school.

Sociologists argue that these patterns can be due to people's home life and what goes on in a school.

WHY THE WORLD IS LIKE A VILLAGE

Sociologists have always been interested in explaining social change. In recent years there have been major social changes, many of which are linked to a process called globalization.

WHAT IS GLOBALIZATION?

In sociology, globalization means that the world is becoming more interconnected. This means that in some ways the world is becoming a smaller place.

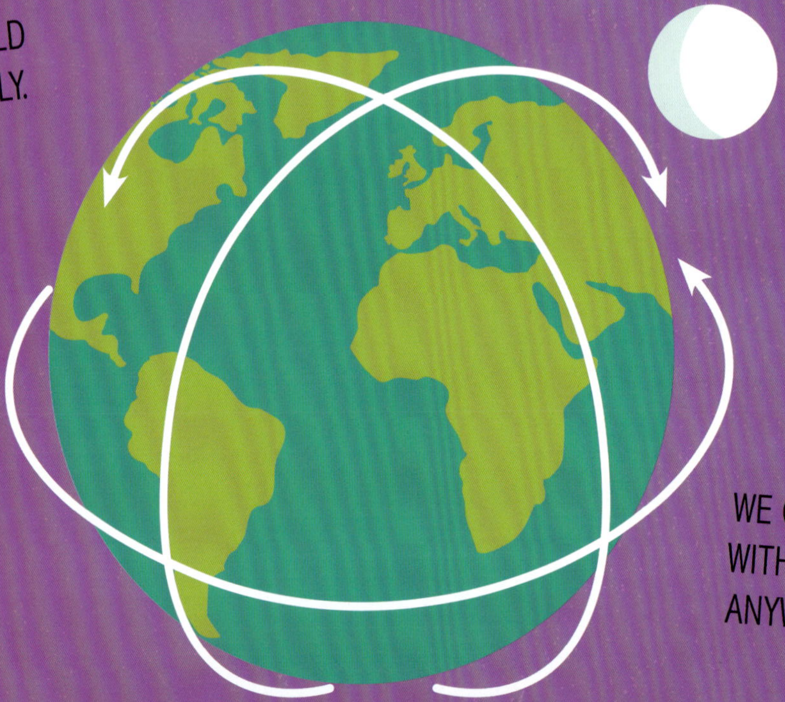

WE CAN TRAVEL AROUND THE WORLD QUICKLY AND EASILY.

WE CAN COMMUNICATE WITH ANYONE, ALMOST ANYWHERE, USING THE INTERNET.

Sociologists are interested in the effects of globalization, for example:

- Ideas about religion and politics spread more easily.
- People can work and live in different places.
- Criminals can go global, and so can the police.
- Businesses can operate in lots of different countries.

PROS AND CONS

Some of these effects are positive and others create problems. For example, if ideas are spreading, some people may feel that their own beliefs may be seen as less important.

One really excellent effect of globalization is that sociologists are becoming more aware of how people from all parts of the world think and how they see the world.

HOW SOCIOLOGISTS CHANGE THE WORLD

As you've seen throughout the book, sociologists play an important part in creating social changes and changes in the law.

SOME OF THESE INCLUDE:

Laws against **racism** and **sexism**.

New laws for crimes against the environment.

Laws to make sure that LGBTQ+ people are treated equally.

THINKING DIFFERENTLY

As well as changes in the law, sociological research is used to make people think differently.

Ideas about **gender** are changing. Gender is the state of being male or female, a combination of both, or neither. Gender is not the same as your biology or the sex you were assigned at birth. There are different ways of expressing your gender identity, or how you see yourself. This means, for example, men may decide to wear clothes that are more feminine in style.

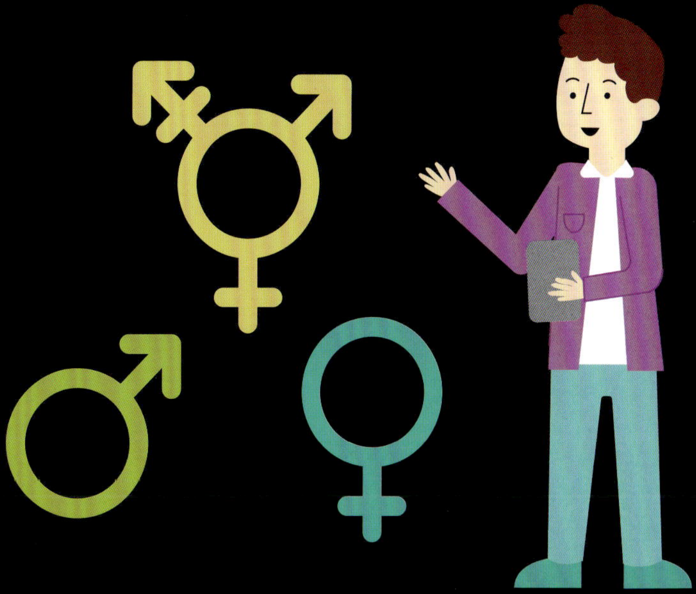

Sociologists help break down stories or myths about people, for example, explaining the contribution that people who move into a country (**immigrants**) make to that country.

Sociologists also point out how policies are needed or need to change. For example, some recent cuts in government spending may have left some groups struggling.

Sociologists carry out research into these effects and campaign for greater fairness in society.

GLOSSARY

Anomie
Normlessness, where there are no clear rules to explain normal behavior

Calvinist
A follower of the Christian teachings of John Calvin, who believed that God controlled all life on Earth

Capitalism
A society that is based on people owning their own property and where trying to make money is seen as important

Communism
A society where the government divides money and property equally

Crime
Any action that breaks a law

Culture
The way of life of a group of people, for example their food, clothes, and beliefs

Demography
The study of the population

Doubly deviant
When women commit crimes, they are seen as criminal and breaking the rules about what it means to be a woman

Empirical evidence
Facts that you can see

Ethnicity
A specific culture or background

Feminist
Someone who wants to make sure there is equality between men and women

Functionalism
The theory that all aspects of a society serve a function and are necessary for the survival of that society

Gender
The state of being male, female, some combination of both, or neither

Globalization
The process whereby the world is becoming increasingly interconnected

Identity
The qualities, beliefs, personality, looks, and/or expressions that make a person or group what they are

Immigrant
A person who moves into a country

Labeling
The process in which meanings are attached to people or behavior

Law
A rule written by a government

Marketization
To run like a business

Marxist
One of a group of thinkers who argue that the way we share goods shapes people's ideas about the world, based on the teachings of Karl Max

Meritocracy
The idea that society is fair and that everyone has an equal chance in education, for example

Myth of meritocracy
People who think that meritocracy doesn't actually exist, that it is a lie

Norms
Something that is usual, or normal

Oppressed
Subject to harsh and unjust treatment

Patriarchy
Male-dominated society

Postmodernist
One of a group of thinkers who believe that other sociological theories are no longer relevant for understanding the world today

Primary research
Research that is carried out for the first time by a sociologist

Qualitative
Research that focuses on meanings and feelings

Quantitative
Research that sees numerical (numbers based) data as most important

Racism
Discrimination based on a person's race

Research
The process by which sociologists gather data

Revolution
Where a group of people fight for massive changes in society

Ruling class
The group of people who own factories and money-making businesses and are in control of the workers

Same-sex
Relating to two men or two women being in a relationship with each other

Secondary research
Research using data that already exists

Sexism
Discrimination based on a person being male or female

Social action theorist
A sociologist who is interested in small scale interactions

Social change
Where ideas and laws adapt over time

Social classes
The division of a society based on social or economic status

Social construct
Something that is built by society, for example, ideas about childhood are socially constructed

Social facts
Values, norms, and structures that exist beyond an individual person

Social movement
A group of people who fight for changes in the law and attitudes

Social problems
Issues that impact many people in a society

Socialization
The process of learning the norms and values of society that take place throughout life

Urbanization
The process where people move from the countryside into towns and cities

Values
Things that are considered to be important in a society

Working class
People who are paid a wage but do not own factories or businesses

FURTHER INFORMATION

BOOKS

The Boy at the Back of the Class (Orion Children's Books, 2018)

The Sociology Book – Big Ideas Simply Explained (Dorling Kindersley, 2015)

Who's in Charge? Systems of Power (series, Franklin Watts, 2020)

WEBSITES

kids.britannica.com/kids/article/sociology/433123
This website has lots of information on sociology and related topics.

www.britsoc.co.uk/what-is-sociology
The website of the British Sociological Association has lots of great information about sociology.

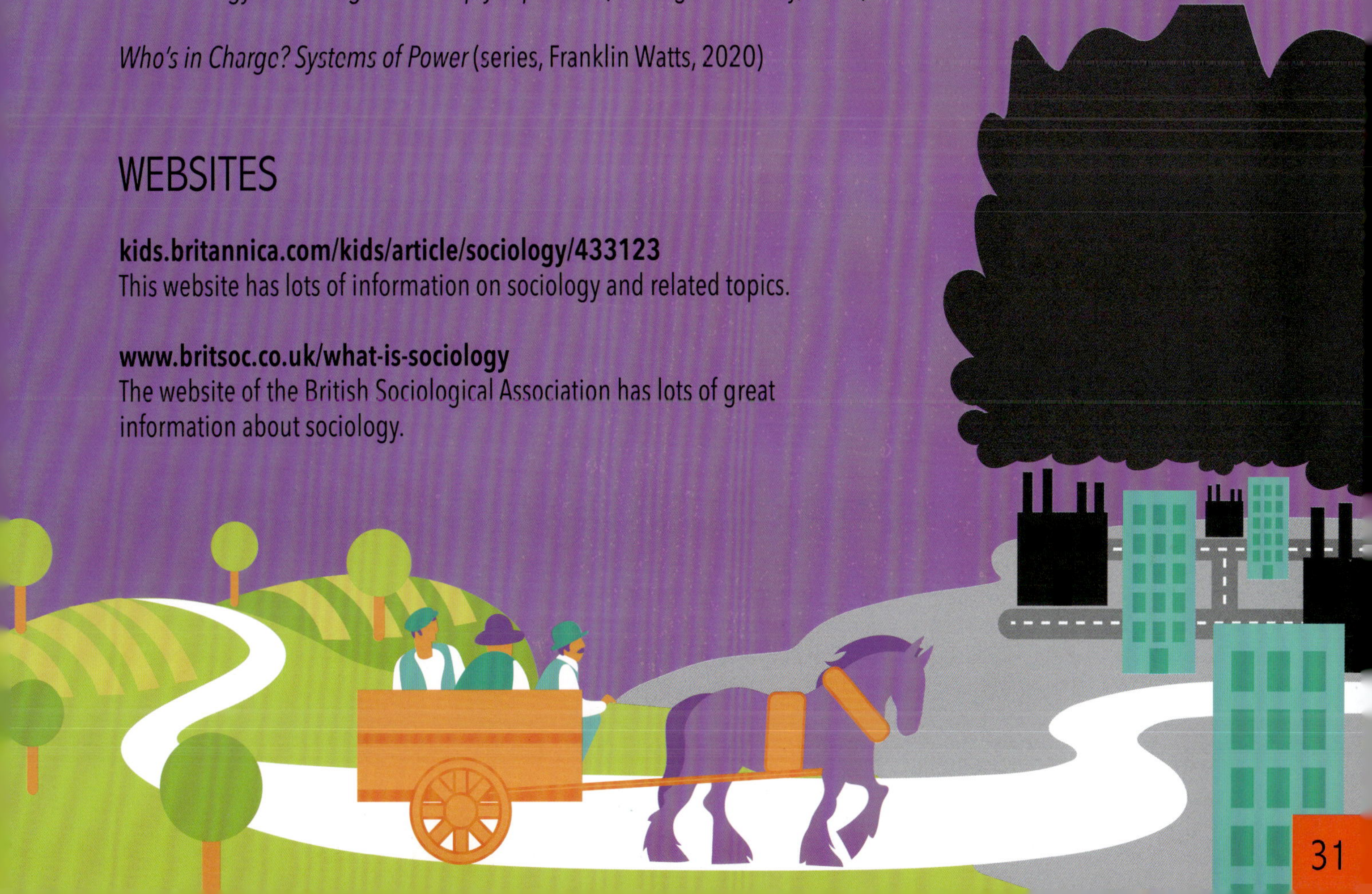

INDEX